Welcome to Excitement, Belief, and Control

by

Don Hodor

*Leslie &
EPic -
Enjoying the fun &
Relationship!
Don &
EPic*

DORRANCE
PUBLISHING CO
EST. 1920
PITTSBURGH, PENNSYLVANIA 15238

Dorrance Publishing Co
585 Alpha Drive
Pittsburgh, PA 15238
Visit our website at *www.dorrancebookstore.com*

ISBN: 978-1-6453-0805-8
eISBN: 978-1-6461-0552-6

Thank you for taking the initiative to read about this concept. By this action, you have singled yourself out as an elite person who is looking for something more in life. Maybe it is a new purpose, mission or re-invention of yourself. Not just financially more, but a growth experience that gives you more fulfillment and reason for living. This concept will help you in many areas including your family, friends, and associates by fulfill their dreams and ambitions as well. I believe your value is based on how you help others with their goals. It may be problem solving, helping with a vision, learning skills, and even spiritual growth. Your goal may be to simply wake up happy and excited about the day ahead or you or it may be to become a key leader in your company, community, family, or with friends. Your first question should be to ask - who is the author? What qualifies the author to be an authority on the subject? How can I believe the author can help me with what I am trying to achieve? What if I don't really know my purpose in life?

I believe I can help you in all of these areas and more. Please allow me to introduce myself and a concept that I have been working on for over thirty years. The interesting fact about this approach is its ability to withstand time and generations. It works just as well with a nine year old to a ninety year old. Believe me, I have been working with a nine year old grandson and a ninety-six year old mother at this time of print. The concept works the same with both.

As a telecommunications engineer, business owner, entrepreneur, and founder/director of a Chamber of Commerce, I have been fortunate to work closely with successful people, mostly business owners. I started in 1976 in the security electronics profession with a startup company of my own using the equivalent of one week's income as my initial investment. At that time I was making a transition as IT Director of a major department store in Pittsburgh and Philadelphia by the name of Gimbel Brothers. I was responsible for all information technology to include over two hundred telephone lines, six hundred POS cash registers online, fire alarms, four hundred CCTV cameras, and associated fire/burglar alarm systems. Along with the technology came executive philosophies, customer demands, and sub-contractors. After ten years in the IT position reporting to the treasurer of Gimbels and a member of the operating board, I decided that the corporate climate and political issues associated were taking too much control of my life. It got to the point of who I had lunch with and who I socialized with in the company had more determination on my future than actual performance and results. I left the company two years before they were sold and eventually closed. My newly formed company specialty was installation of alarm systems, card access systems, and CCTV camera surveillance systems for upscale homes and businesses in Pennsylvania and the tri-state area. More recently, we expanded into VOIP phone systems, internet systems, access control and building cable infrastructure. This quickly brought me to a client base located in the affluent residential and business communities. It was not uncommon to work in homes of 10,000 sq. ft. and larger valued at five million dollars and more. Associated with the executive homes were business leaders who took us into corporate business systems as well. I kept my business small maintaining a one-on-one relationship with my clients. I enjoyed talking with and sharing ideas with this elite group of business leaders. These are top executives of corporations who either owned or were principal executives in the top ranks of their respective companies. When installing security, I worked with the corporate officers to establish how the alarm and camera electronics would fit into their business and lifestyle. As a result, I was intimate with the executive and family lifestyle, concerns, and shared values. Later, I was invited to their business networking parties, cocktail events, happy hours, and morning coffee sessions. I spent many evenings talking about their future plans, goals, and procedures. Often we discussed theories on how to efficiently accomplish those goals. My intent was not to place emphasis on making high profits so much as meeting the right people who were going places and growing by learning about their world with family, friends and business. I wanted to learn about their business and personal philosophy.

Days and months turned into years and soon twenty-five years went by. I stayed in contact with most clients. I met and watched many of them build empires. I also watched many of them go from hero to zero. Rather than study why many failed, I decided to concentrate on those with the highest success. In fact I watched each step, each expansion, changes in their corporations and lives. As they grew, their security, communications, and personal security electronics grew. They went from fax to internet, text, to VOIP phones, remote viewing of office cameras, teleconferencing, etc. Most of them would not make a change or move without calling and meeting to discuss the expansion of information technology in their lives. Ages range from 21 to 92 years old. We'll look at age groups and effect of generational values and how they also impacted daily decisions later in this book. This kept me coming back, sometimes years later, only to pick up on our conversations where we left off. After some time, I had no problem asking about their formulas for success. What was their opinion on how they effectively grew over the years? I enjoyed listening to each theory as everyone wants to tell you how he/she got to a success level. The conversations materialized not just in the office environment, but rather in the intimacy of their homes over cocktails and coffee. Many candid conversations unveiled personal philosophies and how they were orchestrated. I've watched these individuals grow from average people with small businesses to owners of large profitable corporations. I've been intrigued with how these individuals are able to make money, acquire friends, business contacts, and grow quickly. I also experienced their relationships with employees, spouses, family, friends and even enemies. Some were successful financially, but had shipwrecked families coupled with extramarital affairs, legal suits, tax problems, health issues, anger issues and you can only imagine the other problems that can be associated with unchecked growth.

What did I learn about money? <u>I always noticed, money is an amplifier.</u> It makes you more of what your purpose is all about. The greedy get greedier, generous get more generous. Etc.

I decided to focus on the group that "had it together" with family values, money, quality time, and relationships in balance with their financial success. I even looked closely into spiritual values and how they related to the overall growth and satisfaction of the individuals. Some were very religious and some were atheists.

I concentrated my interest on how these people tick. Their ideas and efforts ultimately brought me to writing this book on success concepts. Each person I singled out became a study. I was not shy about discussing and highlighting their success principles. In fact, I openly interviewed each person. My first discovery was most refreshing.

You'll be surprised to know that the old adage "<u>money brings problems</u>" <u>is not true.</u> The saying "money brings problems" may have originated by those without money! Money brings more influence, power, and control over time, values, and direction – not just material accomplishment.

NOTES

NOTES

NOTES

NOTES

PREFACE

What is the secret? What makes average people, sometimes, below average people succeed at great levels? When I was nineteen my cousin Frank Z. insisted I read *How to Win Friends and Influence People* by Dale Carnegie. I practically memorized the book and went around for the next twenty years reading more self-help books and practicing steps, procedures, and endless lists of how to make it happen. I even read the intimidation books and manipulation books in hopes of finding the answer. With my technical background, I was given the gift, sometimes curse, of analyzing every event to the point of saturation in my mind. Too often my wife, friends, and business acquaintances interrupted saying, "Oh! quit analyzing everything!

The big change in my career came when the treasurer of Gimbel's department stores, Dick T said, "Don stop talking in technical terms and just tell me what I need to know in common understandable language." After that advice, I left the nerdy technology and traded it with focus on needs and how to accomplish them. Most of the time it decisions boiled down to "how much cost and how much time?" How quickly can we do it and how well will it work? The old saying, "Don't tell me how to build a watch, I just want to know the time," holds very true.

Now in my senior years, I am still reading self help books and analyzing, but guess what? I found the answer! It's so exciting to find out what life's goals and achievements are about. Now I can share them with you.

Change is changing. We all know about *instant gratification America*: the McDonald's, immediate reward, no waiting syndrome. Amazon, Walmart, and others deliver goods in one day or one hour. Groceries are now delivered to your front door within one hour. Added to this effect is fast information exchange via the Internet, Instagram, Google, Facebook, text, turbo charged advertising, the fast Youtube productions. Movies and TV programs are on demand for immediate viewing when and where we want the experience. Much of this has changed the conventional motivational techniques and put us in a snap decision mode. Often only to change our minds minute by minute.

But what if I don't really know what I want? Goals such as happiness, fulfillment, and self-worth are too vague.

THE CHALLENGE OF WRITING OUR GOALS.

Here is an exercise that will bring light at the end of the tunnel. Let's hope it's not a train coming toward you. Below are questions designed to bring us to focus with pinpoint accuracy the reality of our goals along with suggestions and comments to help us get over this *written goal hurdle*. Don't think in detail about each question listed - quickly pick up a pen and write answers between the questions. Yes, it's okay to write in this book. Be honest, don't think too long or ponder on each answer, be spontaneous.

1. Do I want a better job? Better hours? More understanding boss?

2. Do I like my job? Now ask again, do I <u>really</u> like my job or have I compromised or learned to tolerate?

3. Could I handle my boss's job? If I had *his* job, what changes would I make?

4. Would I own my own business if I didn't have to do paperwork, taxes, invoicing, cash analysis, etc? If I was guaranteed success - What would it be? How could my hobby become a business?

5. Do I have time for my family, friends, and associates?

6. Can I afford to take along family, friends, and associates to educational, recreational, entertaining, and spiritual functions, trips, vacations?

7. Are my vacations compromises, maybe a trip to the brother-in-law's home instead of the beach, in order to save money?

8. Am I having trouble sleeping? Why? Health issues, worry, too hot, too cold, too noisy?

9. If I had an extra $5,000 to spend only on my parents (brother, sister, wife) what would I give them?

10. What car would I like to drive if someone else paid for the purchase?

11. Ever dream of flying an airplane, sailing your own boat, hunting trips, fishing, golfing, going to football, baseball games?

12. When was the last time I took my spouse or family in a limousine for an evening dinner, movie or sports event?

13. Would I like to lose weight? Look younger? Maybe not younger, but healthier? Have time to work out in a gym?

14. If I had an extra $10,000 to give to a church or non-profit charity, what would I present and to what organization?

15. If I had an extra $20,000 I had to give to a friend, who would it be and why?

If none of this is working to get you excited, here is an idea that will jump start your life!

QUESTIONS TO JUMP START YOUR LIFE!

1. Do I have a friend, children, parent that wants a better job?

2. Do my parents, wife, children like what they are doing? Now ask again, do they <u>really</u> like what they are doing?

3. Would I own my own business if I could hire family, close friends, and acquaintances. Would I hire people from my present work place?

4. Does my family, friends, associates have time for me? Do I have time for them?

5. Can they or would they want to go with me on an educational, recreational or entertaining adventure?

6. Where would I take family, friends, or relatives for a vacation if all expenses were paid?

7. How is the health of family, friends, relatives? How can I help them? Do any of them need new glasses, dental, doctor exam, support, advice or counceling?

8. If my family, friends, etc. gave me $10,000 to spend, what would I buy?

9. What car would I like to give to my child, spouse, father, mother?

10. If I could pay for flying lessons, buy a sailboat, plan a vacation, who would I give this gift to?

11. When was the last time my friends took me in a limousine?

12. Would I like my spouse to lose weight? Look younger? Maybe not younger, but healthier?

13. If I could make changes in my church, what would they be?

14. If I had an extra $20,000 for a friend, how would I improve the quality of his or her life?

15. If I'm single, how do I meet the perfect mate? Where? When? How? Who?

By now you're getting the picture! Ask yourself, "If I can't think of goals for myself, why not help others?" You'll feel better, not worry about failure (It's their loss not yours) and contribute to helping those around you.

THREE FACTORS CONTRIBUTE TO THE SUCCESS FORMULA.

I reduced them to three words. It's so simple that it is hard to believe - at first. But if you apply these three simple principles to your everyday life, it will change dramatically. If you're happy where you are, that's better yet. At least you will now recognize the principles and know how to respond. For the first time, you will understand and see how you are being manipulated, controlled, and motivated by others to accomplish tasks that may have not been on your agenda. The three steps in themselves are not significant, but if you place them together sequentially, the results will impress you and others. They will see the change, often instantly! After reading this book, you will spot the effective person, club leaders, group leaders, and pinpoint each component leading up to success. You will see the plot unfold. In most cases, the person or group isn't even consciously aware of their action. In fact, the majority of the time they don't even know the steps they are actually performing. I have been fortunate enough to spend considerable time with multimillionaires to the point many have become close friends. I have confronted these successful people and they are surprised to know of the process when I reveal the steps to them. Most are not aware of the steps they are performing. Sound scary? Not after you understand what is really happening. Many have developed these steps instinctively. Maybe in their DNA, family values, lifestyle or simply copying what their parents, boss or leaders taught them without realizing the source.

I must confess, I really don't like to read but do like the results. I put this 'short' reading book together for the non-reading segment of the population. At the end of each chapter is a summary. Place the information in the kitchen, desk, on the sun visor of the car, on the refrigerator, and in your wallet as a constant reminder. You can even download it to your smart phone or mobile device. It's a good idea to review the principles every few weeks and months to stay on top of your game.

What do you want? Is it money, fame, piece of mind, companionship, health, friends, power? Yes, you have heard this before - set your goals in writing. I learned that this step really can become annoying. This is why writing your goals down is a problem.

Here we go again. We have all heard it. Write down your goals in one, two, five year segments. Be specific. Every author will passionately state the importance of this step. It works. **_Oh really?_** I have my doubts about the procedure. Most of us are very reluctant to actually write down our goals for good reasons. It sounds easy, but let's go through the thinking process.

What stops us from writing and announcing the goals?

1. People will laugh at my goals.

2. If I write them down and do not achieve them, my failure is documented. Now my wife, friends, associates can throw failure back in my face. Most importantly, I will know of my failure and won't like myself.

3. What do I really want? I'm not sure.

4. I'm happy where I am, just need reassurance things won't change. My family and I will keep our health and present status with a retirement that will carry us into our golden years.

5. Change bring unforeseen problems, doesn't it? Something as simple as buying a new cell phones can result in lost calls, phone numbers, misplaced applications, etc.

For many of us, these are valid reasons not to write down our goals. Let's move on and see that each step will help us get what we want. Conclusion; often goals are programmed into our inner self and really don't need to be clarified in writing.

LOVE OF MONEY IS THE ROOT OF ALL EVIL?

By the way, most misquote this as 'money is the root of all evil, not love of money. Let's explore that. Money as a Personality and character amplifier

I like to think of money as a personality and character amplifier. Money allows a person's character to become more intense. He or she becomes more of what their paradigm was before the input of new money. <u>Simply stated, money allows a greedy person to become greedier or a generous person to become more giving</u>. As these people grow in wealth, they assume more control of equipment, time, places, and people around them. Often, more money converts to more opportunity to control more people events and environment. I learned that a generous man who becomes a millionaire is quicker to lend you his Rolls Royce than the lower income man will lend his new lawn mower. A rich man who likes to brag by nature will quickly flaunt his fleet of cars, homes, or executive toys to everyone around him. The poor neighbor across the street is the same guy, just brags about his new barbecue grill or lawn mower. He will make sure his new riding mower is parked in the front lawn every weekend. Conversely, I know generous and wealthy men who actually downplay their material possessions and if unveiled, will ask if you want to borrow any of them. I have driven many of my clients' new Jaguars, Mercedes, and Bentleys. As a licensed airplane pilot, I had the fortune of flying their personal airplanes. This past year, I flew as a guest in a client's private GulfStream Jet for a week in Fort Lauderdale. I watched it happen first hand all too often. An architect friend opened his waterside Chesapeake home for my son's wedding rehearsal dinner. Several friends handed me the keys to their mansions when they went on vacation to use the pool, home theater, or just to hang around and play the grand piano. Yes, generous people with increased wealth do become more generous. On the other side of the coin, I had a very wealthy friend verbally fight over who's paying the lunch tab while his helicopter waited on standby in the parking lot burning hundreds of dollars in fuel.

LET'S TAKE A CLOSER LOOK AT THE WEALTHY

What makes these people so successful? Is it their personality? Do they have a high IQ? Maybe it's their strong work ethic? Long work hours? Is it above average physical characteristics? What really sets these successful people apart as leaders rather than followers? With my technical background as a resource coupled with the number of successful people I met over the twenty-five plus years, I set out to document all aspects of their lives and actions. You ask, "Is this another self-help book?" I too have read dozens of self help books. These books recount stories and offer step-by-step procedures to success, but none really hit the target for me on the simple, concrete essence of success. With my technical background as my tool and logical approach, I got started. I like to find the 'common denominator' when solving a problem. I don't have the time to learn the complicated steps or detailed formulas for success. Let's get to the bottom line quickly and accurately. As I stated earlier, just give me the time, not how to build a watch!

THE SECRET IS IN THREE WORDS.

In this book, I have summarized these success principles into three simple words. This is something you can remember and use daily. I have hit upon the secret and factored all the variables down to the three words. These three words allow each one of us to easily understand the principles. This publication will show you these three simple steps (words), how to recognize them and how to implement them quickly. A recent automobile commercial stated, "There is value in threes" I do believe that is true with this principle. **This is not intellectually difficult, but it is tough to remember to apply them to everyday situations, encounters, conversations, and negotiations.** It takes practice to keep the formula in the front of your mind when meeting and talking to people every day. One suggestion is to write them into your cell phone memo pad or calendar. I have gone so far as to print them and place the sticker on the back of my phone.

This formula works even better when building friendships, business acquaintances, family ties, hobbies, and teamwork events in the office. My conclusion: No, you don't need movie star looks, high intelligence, or any other talents usually associated with success. By the way, those do help. I can almost guarantee you will double or triple your results immediately upon grasping the three-step concept. Just a reminder, I have no scientific credentials or documented studies to back up the information in these pages. I will say that it has worked for me and I have had impressive results making goals easier to achieve. I am highly optimistic this will work for you too. This formula can be adopted to clubs, organizations and non-profit causes, not just individuals.

With all this said, relax and enjoy as you scroll the pages and discover the concept for yourself. If you would like to contact me, please check the information at the end of this publication.

DISCOVERING THE SECRETS

It was there in front of us all the while!

Did you ever look for something only to find it was right in front of you all the while? This is that exact phenomenon. It's been in front of all of us, but now it's suddenly clear. Now you can see the secret principles in three words. You will enjoy going about your day with a new perspective and vivid view as events unfold in front of you with each encounter. You will be able to find, identify each step, and watch the results minute by minute.

Now you can see the secret principles in three words. Let's get started. Here are the three words:

Step 1. EXCITEMENT
Is it exciting?

Step 2 BELIEF/TRUST
Do we believe and trust the person, product, or service?

Step 3 CONTROL
Does everyone clearly understand the investment of time, money, and effort in exchange for the quality and time frame of the reward?

NOTES

NOTES

NOTES

Chapter One

Excitement

Let us take inventory by starting with you.

Are you exciting? Are your surroundings exciting? Are your business associates and friends exciting? What draws attention to you? The next time you are with a group of people take notice; Is there one particular person or couple in the room that others are drawn to? While driving on the highway, which signs draw attention the most? Which cars draw your attention? When watching TV, what draws your attention? The same question should be asked while reading magazines, listening to music, shopping, dining, movies, etc. All are opportunities to see the three words being acted out.

Excitement puts us all in a hypnotic state. Excitement usually appeals to a person's ego and pride. Most of the time it induces an emotional state. Sometimes it can appeal to the nobler motives such as religious beliefs and character. Most often I stick with ego and pride a recognizable force in our society.

Let's re-state the question? What draws our attention?

Answer: Anything that is exciting.

That sounds interesting, but really, what exactly is exciting? What gets us excited? Let's start with the dictionary definitions.

Key

1. To stir to activity.

2. To call forth (a reaction or emotion, for example) elicit

3. To arouse strong feeling in: speakers who know how to excite a crowd.

4. Physiology. To produce increased activity or response in (an organ, or part) stimulate.

5. Physics: To increase the energy of. To rise to a higher energy level.

I like the definition: raising the level of expectation and awareness. Putting people's minds in motion. Creating energy in thinking, actions, decisions and goals.

Now an even better question. How can I help make excitement work for you?

The following tools will help you and others get excited. Increasing excitement around you will get you even more excited as well. It is contagious and builds in a group of two or more. As an exercise, first, let's get others excited by making them feel important and genuinely increase their purpose especially if it matches our goals at the same time. Here are some categories that generate excitement:

POWER
MONEY
SEX
HUMOR
FEAR

DANGER

SADNESS

HAPPINESS

EMOTIONS THAT ARE NEGATIVE: ANGER, MAD, DIS-
APPOINTED, THREATENED, RESENTMENT, EMBARRASS-
MENT

Let's take each of these classifications of excitement and demonstrate examples of how we can use them to get others excited (and motivated) around us.

POWER:

Most people think of power as the ability to control other people.

Common statements we hear repeated about power include:

He knows a lot of influential people.

He can pick up the phone and get things done.

He has the connections.

These statements are commonly associated with power. Power (and perceived power) makes a person exciting. Our increased number of acquaintances, business contacts and talented resources equates to power.

MONEY:

Power is often associated with money. What makes money powerful? Let's not kid ourselves on the subject of money. The obvious: money can buy action with labor, control time, access to special equipment, cars, airplanes, higher quality environment, and to some extent, create loyalty. How many of us have stayed with a company because it offers a great retirement plan? That is buying long-term loyalty. We always hear money isn't everything or money can't bring happiness. It can do a lot for us if we know how to convert it to our goals.

What makes money exciting?

It's the ability to convert or exchange or buy quickly into so many actions, products, or services. This is obviously exciting. Many can be financially rich with a big bank account but unable to spend it on their lifestyle and goals. Money raises the level of expectation around the people who have money if it is converted to excitement. After all, any tool that controls our time, space, or quality of existence is exciting. Money can do that easily. Let's look at a typical day and how money can solve many problems.

Don't like to cut the grass or take the garbage out? Hire a gardener.

Don't like to do housekeeping or laundry? Hire a maid or dry cleaner.

Don't like to drive in traffic? Hire a chauffer.

Don't like to wait in lines at grocery stores? Have a delivery service do the job.

Don't like checking into the airport? Buy a private jet or helicopter.

Want to lose weight? Hire a dietician, nutritionist, cook, and contact a personal trainer.

Are your kids keeping you occupied too much? Causing your to loose quality time wth your spouse? Hire a nanny. Hire a sports instructor for them. (Golf, tennis, etc.)

Got health issues? Hire the best doctors and medical treatment.

Now that we used money to take care of all those routine daily problems above, you can focus on the more important things in life. For instance, spending quality time with those you care about most. Now you can follow the goals you are most passionate about.

Warning: The one thing money cannot control!

<u>The one thing money cannot control is the 'free will' of another person</u>. Money can heavily influence free will but cannot ultimately control it. In fact, it's been said that free will is the one thing even our creator cannot control within us. A complete book was written about the subject of 'free will' of about 788,000 words - the Bible.

Before we go into more detail about people with money, I would like to clarify an observation I have seen firsthand. Many people may not have money (they are cash poor) but they may have access to people in power. They may have access to tools such as limousines, jets, helicopters, yachts, country clubs, vacation condos, media, luxury cars, etc. They may control machinery and equipment such as factory tooling, transportation, technology, communication media (newspaper, radio, TV, internet), and more. They have access to a wealthy lifestyle and wealthy people. Some have law enforcement or political access. We often hear the statement, "I heard he/she is financially broke or bankrupt." At the same time, we note that he or she has power. Power but no money? The bankruptcy issue may or may not be true but if the individual has access to tools and powerful people on a regular basis, they have access to power or wealth and the ability to convert these to excitement. They have access to lifestyle and wealthy people and have been empowered from another source.

There is one tool that all of us can access with great results. Social Media. How many have organized demonstration groups, good and bad projects by simply using the internet with Facebook, Instagram, websites, e-mail campaigns, publications, etc. We now live in an era when anyone with a smart phone can post a video, picture, or recorded conversation and broadcast it to the world with a click. This is a new power that is allowing anyone on the social and economic scale to have power. Concepts true or false can excite and motivate people. We should all be aware that we are all ***online*** with CCTV cameras, recordings, and hidden equipment everywhere and always. Always act as if someone is watching – because they most likely are.

Let's explore conventional excitement generation tools. Here are a few example of excitement generating tools:

A person or group arrives in a limousine. That act alone raises emotions revolving around power and money. You may say, "I don't have a limousine." For that important occasion, rent one. Very few people, wealthy or poor, have experienced the comfort and convenience of a limousine night on the town. (Weddings, proms, and funerals don't count. Too many are crowded into the limo to get a full effect) Try a limo if you want to get your friends, clients, spouse, or family excited.

Another example of an excitement generating tool: A yacht brings with it excitement, belief, and control. The captain and owner have control over the passengers, time, space, and destination. You may say, "I can't afford a yacht." Consider a timeshare, split partner owners, charter, or if you're lucky, borrow one from a friend. Very few people, wealthy or poor, have experienced the comfort and convenience of taking a private yacht on an island shoreline cruise. We're not talking about a cruise ship, but a private yacht with captain and convenience of controlling your own trip schedule as to when and where you want to go to as a destination. It can be as simple as a sailboat, powerboat, or even a canoe. Try this if you want to get your clients, friends, spouse, or family excited.

SEX APPEAL:

Sex appeal can be one of the most exciting tools, even more effective than money and power. Many philosophize that sex is the driving force that gets us up in the morning - the reason we work and the underlying theme when we play. It is obviously exciting. Many tools project sexual excitement such as stylish clothes, watches, jewelry, shoes, a tan, thin body, hairstyle, sun glasses, etc. Sex appeal can also come with humor, gestures, concern over one's attitude, compliments, expectations, and imaginary stories in casual conversation.

ENTERTAINMENT - TALENT

Excitement can be found in the form of entertainment. Who doesn't like to laugh and have fun, enjoy music, watch a sports figure, movie star, etc.? It allows us to fight boredom and forget our pains, complaints, fears, anxieties, and sadness. A good comedian, professional or amateur, is always the center of excitement. Talents with music, sports, art, or singing are all exciting. It's a good idea to learn to play a musical instrument, sing, or perform and speak in front of a group. Take a speaking class. If you can't do this, remember you can hire someone who can perform for you for your special event. One word of caution, humor is usually at the expense of someone else's values. Watch who's toes you are stepping on.

FEAR, DANGER, SADNESS:

I have grouped these words together in a category that I'll refer to as anticipated or real <u>loss</u>. No one wants to lose power, sex, money, or fame. The fear of these losses and consequences is in itself exciting or at least stimulating. It can motivate us. We will examine the contract between gain (goals and achievements) and pain (loss or setback) and how the two add amplification or power to the excitement formula.

Phrases we hear every day that bring out excitement that are founded or formulated around the gain-pain principle:

> Sale ends today
> Limited offer
> Only a few qualify
> This is your last chance
> Be the first... Act now
> Save money now, don't wait

7

Don't be left out

Don't be sorry

All of these imply that you are in a special, important position to make a decision of gain and if you don't act now you can lose that opportunity. TV commercials are designed to lure us into an excited state. Statements such as, "*If you don't act on this opportunity now, you will lose out*" are common. Advertisers present a product value tied in with limited time offer or limited number of products, customers, or locations. They often put a qualifier to the deal such as age, geographical area, size, intelligence, limited quantity, availability, income level, credit worthiness, etc. How do we stimulate these emotions and how do we convert these feelings into excitement with action and goal oriented results? A simple esample such as, "If we don't leave now, we will miss the movie and this is the last showing." That works to get others around us moving.

Some of the obvious and not so obvious motivators:

1. Act now, limited offer

2. Only a few left

3. We close this offer at the end of the week

4. Only qualified prospects can apply

5. We will be sold out

6. The first XX get a special prize

7. Win a gift with each purchase

8. Prices are going up

9. This is the lowest price we will offer

On the other side of the formula:

1. I'll shop for lower prices

2. I can go to another brand instead of this one

3. I am making an offer of $XX but will drop the offer at end of business day.

4. I can only wait one day to hear your acceptance

5. I really don't need your product.

6. Price is too much

7. I can't wait that long – I'll go somewhere else.

8. I'll report your activity or mishandling to your management

9. I'll post your unfair practices on the internet

10. If I like this product/service, I can bring you more business with friends, associates, etc.

11. How much if I buy quantities?

12. How much if I pay cash now

EXCITEMENT TURN-OFFS

Sloppy, wrinkled clothes

Poor grooming

Equipment or automobile that is dirty or in bad repair

Poor eye contact

Making people wait

Not returning phone calls, texts, or emails in a timely manner

Complaining or excuses without adding positive help with ideas

Slow when responding to questions or speaking

Slow movement or actions

In general, are your actions slow, old, repeated, motionless, confusing, or hard to follow? Details such as bad posture, talking too low, bad breath can add to avoidance. Those are the signs that can cause others to walk away. The opposite of excitement is boredom or inactivity.

EXCITEMENT TURN- ONS

Nice stylish clothes with a good fit

Good grooming

Clean automobile

Candor, honesty, trustfulness

These actions draw people to us.

Summary on excitement: Do we look exciting, surround ourselves with excitement, speak with excitement? These actions cause us to get closer to the person or group.

Ask yourself. What is exciting about your product or service in business?

Word of caution: You can be doing all the steps correctly on the checklist but you are rejected by the group leader. Often this is because the leader sees that you are more exciting and as a result you are taking control of his group or project. He or she will recognize the talent and try to remove you from the group. You will be set up to fail. Tactics include misinforming you of the goals, not telling you when the next meeting is scheduled, not giving you time in front of the group, deliberate assignment of menial tasks to keep you away from the core objective, taking credit for your ideas, and attacking your character behind your back.

When you are confronted with this situation, you are often left with few alternatives. The existing leader usually has control of the finances and you do not. What are your options? Point out the leadership flaw to others? This is difficult as the existing leader has established his or her leadership using existing (maybe old or boring) concepts that worked in the past. New ideas bring challenges, changes, and a different way of thinking that are often rejected by the status quo group. Maybe consider leaving the group and starting your own?

NOTES

NOTES

NOTES

Chapter Two
Belief/Trust

What is trust, also referred to as belief? How do we get people to believe in us? How do we get people to believe in our products or services? How do we project belief in our business? How do we acquire trust in our relationships? The list is endless. The action of belief ties in closely with trust. What we are really asking is, Do I trust you? Do I trust your claims? Do I trust that your product will work? - And most importantly, <u>Do I trust that you and your product or service will work for me</u>?

One of the simplest explanations is with a weight loss product. As we watch the commercial we are asking: Do I believe he or she really lost weight with the diet plan? Do I believe the product will work for me? Do I believe I have the discipline to perform the task necessary to lose the weight (might be exercise, food choices, drink mix, pills, etc.)? Do I believe in the person or products? Do I believe I can follow through? You can see how belief (trust) transfers from messenger (salesman) to the product (lean body formula) or service to the person (you). As you can see, belief has many components that need addressed when moving forward.

THE FIRST STEP TO PROJECTING BELIEF.

Be genuine and sincere. If you are selling a weight loss product or service, you better be losing weight! Do I believe? Do I trust? Why or why not?

TRUST GENERATING TOOLS

We generally trust name recognition. That is why so much is spent on advertising and using well-known people who are easily recognized. This means (as mentioned earlier) dress code, good grooming, clean automobile, speaking clearly, and making eye contact. Be genuine and sincere. Example: Even if you know a person, when calling always say, "Hi this is (your name). Do you have time now?" That simple statement brings more familiarity and trust each time the called person hears it. We generally thrust conservatively-dressed people. Wear a sport coat, tie, and light colors when possible. Oh, but you say casual dress allows you to relate better to the customer. Remember the customer wants trust in the company, product, and service. Not just a casual friend.

Most people trust recognized symbols. Examples are the U.S. flag, Coke, Nike, and name brand products in general. We generally trust people who work in established offices in quality buildings. Think about meeting a banker who is dressed in shorts and a t-shirt standing in a mobile motor home versus a banker who is wearing a suit and tie in a brick office building. Which one would you trust with your money?

Length of time in business is important? Who are your clients? These are tips you should be using.

These are just a few of the images we notice and how they relate to belief and trust.

Belief as an action: It all starts with the first meeting. Was he or she on time? Did he remember details about me? Did she remember my name? Did he remember our past conversations? Did she remember what I came here for? Did he follow up with his promise to deliver? He said, "I'll bring donuts to the meeting." Did he? She said, "I'll bring you that article we talked about." Did she? We start with the little promises and use them as building blocks toward establishing belief and trust on the bigger items.

Sidebar: Here is a simple test when evaluating trust and belief in a person: How do they treat others in subordinate positions? How do they talk with waiters, doorman, bellhop, cab drivers, etc.? Respect for others ties in closely with trust and belief. The two traits are closely related. Be careful with people around you who treat others with disrespect. This is an indication of whether or not we can trust the persons 'respect' with our time, quality of life, and space. I always like to watch how associates handle greeters, waiters, and cleaning help. Do they talk down to them? Are they disrespectful? This is a good indicator of the associates respect for a fellow human being, including you.

THIRD PARTY TESTIMONIES AS A TOOL

Another tool used to project belief and trust is <u>third party testimonials</u>. Always have a customer list of endorsements on record or a list of customers that will take a call or write a letter for reference. Ask for a letter and keep it on file with your literature. Your future clients should be able to ask how customers feel about your company, attitude, product, or service. Did we deliver what was expected? On a social level, referring to existing friends or acquaintances often works well.

The Western Pennsylvania trust quiz: These three questions appear to be a part of the Western, Pennsylvania business culture. The following three questions are cues or indicators that the future customer, friend, or associate is looking for a solid trust foundation.

- Where do you live? Where is your work place?

17

- How long have you lived here? (Worked here?)

- Who do you know that I know?

When you hear these questions, you know the party is looking for trust.

TITLES AS A TOOL

We generally trust people with titles: president, vice president, treasurer, officer. But beware: who appointed the title? Was it a group, club members, corporate management, or was the title self appointed? Many banks are aware of this building block and appoint everyone as a vice president.

AWARDS AS A TOOL

We generally believe in awards: first place, best sales, best quality, largest dealer, top salesman, employee of the month. But beware: who gave the award? Was it a group, a club, group peers, chamber of commerce, or was the award self appointed. Best hot dog in town? By who's standard or vote? Car dealer service centers like to cover the walls with service awards. They know it works.

Automobiles as tools: Many will say, "I won't drive a luxury car. It's a turn off." This is not a true statement. In most cases, your friend, associate, or client may not like a luxury car because they are envious, see the expense as unnecessary, or feel intimidated. But they do respect what it represents. Power, excitement, and maybe belief that you can afford the lifestyle associated. We know they do respect what it represents. You can neutralize the effect by picking a color such as navy blue, white, or silver. Beware of black or dark tinted windows as it can send a message of distrust. If you can't afford a new luxury car, pick something that is three to five years old and make sure to keep it clean and shiny. At times you project a more trusting image with an older clean Mercedes or BMW than a newer dirty, unkempt Chevy. Remember to be humble, don't brag. Others are looking at the total package, you and how you handle the possession. For special occasions, consider renting a car or borrowing one from a friend. One factor has shifted to trucks instead of cars. A pickup truck projects honesty, genuine qualities, and a hard worker. Make sure it's kept clean and in good shape.

NOTES

NOTES

NOTES

Chapter Three

Control

Of the three words - <u>control</u> is the most challenging. Missing this step is what often leads to divorce, lawsuits, lost sales, bad feelings, split friendships, or lost opportunity. Lack of control is the primary reason business partnerships fail and where the big mistakes are made. Often people ask me, "Doesn't control sound negative?" Control can sound negative as in, "He is controlling my every move. He is a control freak. He always has to be in charge."

Many think that control or controlling is a bad idea or statement. In truth, control is necessary. However, it should be fair to all parties. A win-win approach is needed. The reality is controls are only negative if they are unfair. Conversely controls must be fair to all parties involved in order to work. All parties should understand the requirements and exchanged value from the beginning of a deal or project to the end. The deal should be fair to all and stated clearly up front.

Here is a simple example that we encounter in our everyday lives. Let's say you are going on a date but are not sure of the other person's intentions. For the ladies, going on a date should be accompanied with a statement, "Yes, you can take me to the movie. I'll in return cook a dinner at my house next week." Now there is no misunderstanding as to what the guy gets in return for the movie ticket and evening companionship. Most of us are embarrassed to state the traded value up front and think it is a turn off or deal breaker to bring up the control factor. The real turnoff is not knowing the exchange of value or outcome. With the date, the guy may have thought a romp in bed was his reward for the movie. She took control by forecasting the outcome of the date before the event got its start.

Here is another example of what can go wrong without proper control. Let's just look at the simple task of hiring someone to clean our car. Joe is the neighbor kid who is looking for odd jobs for the summer. We ask Joe if he is willing to wash the car for $10. We shake hands and the process begins. This approach is going to be a problem. We go outside two hours later only to see that the car was not touched. When we find Joe, he states, "Oh, Mr. Neighbor, I was planning on doing that tomorrow morning." The price was established but the quality of work, time frame, and quantity of work were not defined. We both lost control of the deal. What is the best approach? First go over the car with Joe and write down a checklist of what is expected. Wash the car this afternoon, clean the tires, towel dry the car, clean the windows, vacuum the inside and wipe down the seats. Write this down on a pad while walking Joe around the car. Now attach the $10 bill to the bottom of the page. Mention that payment will be upon completion of the check list. If we gave the money to Joe but failed to list the items in detail, we do not have a valid contract and we lost control of the outcome. We can't complain of the quality, dirty windows, or crumbs on the floor if the contract is not written. In this case a simple note on a pad is sufficient and keeps us all in control.

So many misunderstandings come up between friends, customers, clients, relationships because the <u>exchange</u> was not discussed clearly up front or put in writing. That is why a contract is needed. Control requires a contract. The contract can be verbal statements with both parties agreeing with a handshake, written notes, check list or actual legal document.

How do we fix this problem? Let's go to dinner, I'll buy. Let's go to dinner you pick the restaurant and you buy. Hummmm. At least you don't have that awkward moment when the check arrives. Let's go to dinner and go Dutch? We must have control and we must have a contract in order to meet the goals successfully without misunderstandings on either side of the agreement. This can be verbal but should be written, even if it's an informal notepad approach. The best way to establish the deal is to follow-up with a text to the person you are involved with. This can be in the form of a follow-up email, txt or written outline. For bigger business deals, don't be afraid to ask for a non-circumvent, non-disclosure, non-compete document to be signed at the onset. Then no one can say and idea, deal, or concept was taken or stolen from another party. This approach has become common today. If the other party would say something like, " My word is good enough", your response is, " yes, I trust your word but one of us may become ill or even die."

Key points to keeping control of the relationship, service or product.

1.   What is to be completed as a task?

2.   What is the price?

3.   When does the job begin and end?

4.   What is the listing of service or product to be delivered?

5.   Who is performing the services?

6.   When does the payment(s) and amounts take place?

7. What is the guarantee if applicable?

For a date or dinner out:

1. Where are we going?

2. Who is paying?

3. When do we meet?

4. What happens after the dinner?

5. What happens if someone is late? i.e. text your arrival time.

6. Send RSVP reminders or confirmation.

7. Ask "Please update me of any time changes."

Those parameters listed above will help to keep control of the project. We must clearly understand what the exchange will consist of for all parties in the deal. There are different types of contracts we often don't realize exist. For example:

People: Verbal agreements, a handshake. A 'to do' list, Posting rules or procedures.

In sales use a printed receipt, sales agreements, invoices, letters of agreement or letters of understanding. It's always a good idea to send a follow-up email highlighting the meeting and what is expected of each party.

Product: Specifications, warranties, test results

Service: Final inspections, passing test scores, quality control checklists. The formula: No contract = no control = misunderstanding and disappointment. We enter into casual contracts all the time and don't realize it. When getting a parking garage ticket, read the back. It's a contract. When entering a parking garage, you agreed to the contract when you pushed the button to accept the ticket. Printed statements such as, "Not responsible for stolen items", "driver must pay full amount if ticket is lost", "do not park in reserved spaces or lot closes at midnight" - this is in effect a contract that is usually printed on the back of the parking ticket. When you enter a hotel swimming pool or tennis court, you see a sign posted: To use this facility please read the rules - you must adhere to these rules, etc. You entered into a contract the minute you set foot in the pool or court.

What is the most common contract mistake?

What is it the most critical and often repeated mistake in making a deal (contract)?

Most of us forget the time element when using controls. How long will it take to deliver the goods or services? How long will it take for payment? In today's business world, thirty day net is expected unless spoken or addressed on the work order or invoice. Printing on an invoice, payment due upon receipt can move cash quickly.

IS THIS CONTROL ELEMENT A CHRISTIAN PRINCIPLE?

The question often comes up, Are these principles Christian in nature? What if I have Christian values? What if I don't?

Let's go through the checklist.

Was Jesus Christ exciting?

With miracles, lessons, and teachings he gathered crowds who were obviously excited to see and hear him. He offered the best product/service known to mankind - the message of eternal life!

Was Christ believable – could we trust him?

With his miracles and actions, his twelve disciples and others believed and trusted him.

Editorial: This can get tricky with so many opposing viewpoints from different beliefs and religions. Many claim there is no positive proof of his existence, death, or return to life. The belief must be based on simple faith.

Let's get to the bottom line - Did Christ have control?

I had a hard time finding the control aspect of Christianity at first. Then I met a Christian book author who brought the answer to light. Once again, it was right in front of us. The Bible is a document (contract) for guidance in our daily living. In writing, it outlines what we are to do, our acceptance of the deal, how we are to live, and what our reward will be. These principles and procedures are revealed in the Ten Commandments, written stores about forgiveness and belief, examples, and promises. If acceptable, the reward provided "in writing" is eternal life after death. It's all controlled in a written contract to all of us - The Bible. It can be found in other religious documents such as the Koran, Old Testament, etc.

WHAT ABOUT NON-CHRISTIANS?

The excitement, belief, control process works outside of Christianity and other faiths as well. Let's say you are robbed at gunpoint. Certainly this is not a Christian principle but do the three words work?

Excitement = A gun pointing at you

Belief = Will the robber pull the trigger? Is it a real gun and is it loaded? Do we trust he will use it on us?

Control = What options do I have? What options does the gun holder have?

All the elements of a deal are present without Christian principles to make it work. What is the exchange? My life for my money - simple. It's a deal.

This is a universal three step process that works. Excitement, belief, control, and how it relates to deception versus good will. Either way the principle works.

IS THIS A MANIPULATION TOOL?

Interestingly it can be used either way, but works better if you are genuine in your approach. The work and reward should be mutually beneficial to all parties. I am not suggesting that you lie or build up false images of what and who you are. These tactics will work in the short term but when building long-term relationships, they will backfire and fail. In the case of the robber, you will remember his face and when and if you see him again, you will back out of the deal! People are not very forgiving when they have been deceived. That is the ultimate insult to our intelligence, moral values, and sense of fair play. You can pretend to be someone you are not, but sooner or later you will have trouble keeping the image. It's harder work to project a false image then it is to perform the hard work.

BEING SINCERE, COUPLED WITH
EXCITEMENT, BELIEF, AND CONTROL WORKS BEST BY FAR.

Here are a few friends and associates and how they handled the three-word program.

Meeting Àngelo

Being in the security alarm business, I was asked to give a quote for equipment to be installed in Angelo's house. A third party referred me, so I had no idea who I was visiting. As I pulled up the long driveway, I could see a spacious stone home resembling a small castle in architectural design. It looked to be built in the late 1940s with workmanship that could not be easily duplicated by today's tradesmen making it priceless. Each stone was systematically placed reflecting the great pride of workmanship that only meant hard work and talent of past stone masons.

The perimeter border of the property and driveway had a secure feel with large tall black iron fencing. As I came up the driveway, I stopped at a large gated barrier that resembled the entrance to an eccentric estate. After waiting for a few minutes, a caretaker came to my window and asked, "Do you have an appointment?" I gave him my card and he opened the gate. Driving in, I noticed all the trees and plants were neatly trimmed in a pattern of geometric shapes that only meant that much care was taken with gardener's pride of workmanship. The driveway snaked to the back of the house revealing a large, finely landscaped lawn unfolding below. I then turned down another long driveway that descended on a terrace with a large swimming pool. Beside the pool was a matching smaller stone house with a tiled roof. It looked to be an old carriage house that was converted to a pool cabana. As I turned behind the pool cabana a twelve car garage appeared in view. Each garage door had nine glass panes with richly varnished wood frames. Inside I could faintly see several Rolls Royce's, a Mercedes convertible, and many vintage automobiles.

I stepped out of my car and entered a small walk-in gate to the pool area. Setting in a recliner chair under a large bright green umbrella was a well-tanned middle-aged gentlemen with dark sunglasses and a phone in his hand. He motioned for me to be seated but continued to talk a lengthy time on the phone. I only heard his side of the conversation, but it was clear that he had no problem with my listening. In fact he seemed to talk louder and staring at me the same time as if I was part of his conversation. It was obvious he wanted me to hear his business deal. He was talking to someone in Florida and discussing a business merger. He threw out many clichés such as: We'll make lots of money together, let's fly to Las Vegas to celebrate, etc. I have never heard a conversation at this level other than in the movies. After what felt to be twenty minutes, he abruptly ended the conversation and turned to me with questions.

Do you like what you're was doing for a living?

Are you making the money you want and are you interested in making more?

What are your annual sales?

Would you like to make more?

What model/year car are you driving?

I was taken back. I thought this was a sales call for electric gates, intercom, etc.

His questioning immediately opened two thoughts.

1. He seemed to be interested in helping me make more money.
2. He appeared to want to employ me or partner in business.

Keep in mind, I only came to quote a price for installation of motorized gates and an intercom system. We'll step back into the details of the sale, but I must move forward and convey that after leaving, I was excited. I immediately went home to my wife and told her about the experience. He was the first man to express an interest in helping me get rich. He stated that his initial reaction was that he liked me and wanted to help me move forward in life. I was excited about his approach and given the opulent surroundings believed and trusted he was one of the few I met in life that could possibly help me. Yes, the venue was <u>exciting,</u> <u>I trusted the wealth was real,</u> and just maybe he would help me to have <u>control</u> of my future.

We didn't spend much time with details about the motorized gate, intercom system, or telephone system. He only stated, "Give me your best system at the best price and we can do business together." He brought up the possible use his home as a model and that he would introduce me to his many high-end friends and clients. They would buy from me upon his recommendations. Upon the return trip. I did present a very nice system and a discounted price. Upon presentation of the system and cost, he stated, "This is good. Let's start," and he added, "We will get rich together as partners." I asked for a down payment, upon which he responded, "This is not just a down payment on the system quoted, but rather one of a series of investments in your company." After finishing the installation of a motorized gate, intercom to the house and pool, and remote control to open and close the gate, I presented the final bill. Instead of paying me, he handed me the keys to a new top model Cadillac and said, "Take it home, use it for a few weeks, and see how the wife likes it." This car was way beyond my financially affordable transportation but I took the keys and glided home in this bright burgundy model. I pulled into the driveway of my home and waited anxiously for my wife to look out the window.

Finally after dinner, my wife left the dog out and returned to ask, "What's with the Cadillac?" I explained the whole adventure and took her for a ride in what was her first luxury car experience. Although not materialistic by nature, she did point out the safety aspect for the kids and anticipated reliability. She did remember Angelo's name from that day forward. That was twenty years ago. I still remember the first day I met Angelo as if it were yesterday. I still do considerable business with the Angelo company and he would continue to promise to get rich with me up until his death a few years ago. Yes, I jumped to his service expecting that day to come. He had a high degree of control over me using the mystic power by exciting me into believing he is my pot-of-gold at the end of the rainbow. We did do business together and although he died a few years ago, I often go back to his principles. Do we need a fancy home, pool, Rolls Royce to control the outcome of the relationship? No, but it does help if you have these tool for excitement. Remember, people always gravitate to a goal-oriented dreamer over a mundane person without sharing vision.

Meet Frank

Frank is a client who became a friend over the years. Frank used an entirely different technique for getting people around him excited. His excitement technique was one of using <u>detail</u> as a tool. I walked into his office off the street using a cold call technique. Asking, "Is your phone system working up to your expectations?" His receptionist asked me to return the next day for an appointment to go over a quote for a new telephone system. The next day when I arrived fifteen minutes early, I was asked to wait. Within a minute of our quoted appointment time, he had me escorted into his conference room where he had several proposals laid on a table. He asked me to look at all of them and provide a detailed evaluation of each and to glean any ideas from them. He also asked that I contribute any insight into design of the telephone system. This was the first time and only time a client used this approach to getting a purchase quote. He kept me excited by adding extreme detail to the proposal. Questions like sample of colors of the phones. What was the exact layout of the keys and buttons? What was the weight of the receiver and how it compared to competition? What was the physical size of the phone? How did the ringer sound? What was the schedule of payment? What were the names of the employees who were going to install the system? Did I have a copy of my insurance liability, workman's compensation, and corporate papers? These details caused me to take many extra steps never taken before. Needless to say, Frank kept me focused and excited about the sale. I have been doing business with Frank and his company for about thirty years now and he kept my attention by focusing in on great detail.

Frank and his wife invited my wife and me to his yacht which he kept in the Bahamas. Each year he would fly us, all expenses paid, to spend a week with him and his wife. One evening while sipping on a glass of wine he was seated on the captain chair at the head of the deck table marked "Chairman of the Board" on the back.

I asked, "I have watched you go from a trailer office to four dealerships. Frank, what is your secret?

His quick response was, "Don, I always pay attention to details."

I asked, "How you can do that with such a large company?" Isn't it about the 'big picture' and not micro managing your staff?

His response, "It's easy, the big picture for everyone in the company is to pay attention to details."

We later talked about his system and analyzed it in detail. We noticed some employees gloss over and forget all the product details. At the same time we noticed that these same employees know every player, standing, and position in the March Madness basketball finals. But, They forget detailed specifications on his inventory of truck and trailers. We found that it all boils down to where compassion and excitement comes into play. We tend to re-member details when excitement is coupled with details. The key is to find what excites us about a product, system, career, or agenda. By the way, there are techniques that will add detail. One simple trick is to write everything down at meetings, etc.

Looking back Frank used infinite detail to keep everyone around him ex-cited, in focus, and in control. Our visit to Franks yacht came with a detailed set of instructions. The instructions included a calendar outlining events and what to pack for the trip. Type of clothing, light jackets for cool breezy nights, toiletries, etc. Upon arriving at the yacht, detailed instructions were placed by each bedside listing all the schedule and procedures. (do not open windows, laundry drop off, for safety no socks as floors were slippery, etc.) Each day started with an announcement as to what was being scheduled, walking the beach in the morning, coffee break at 10:30 AM, clean up for lunch, noon to 1 PM, jet ski boating from 2 PM to 4 PM. Staying with the schedule and working with the details outlined kept us excited and in control during the entire vacation. This also kept his crew focused on tasks and what to expect while serving all of us. Moving to his corporate environment, I noticed low turnover of employees. When I asked how this was accomplished, he gave a simple but detailed answer. Each employee had a retirement plan, profit sharing linked to performance, and a reward program based on years factored with position and sales growth. If you left the company before retirement age, a portion of the profit sharing was held back and shared with those that stayed. It all worked fine for Frank's business and with the micro-details, he could spot someone slacking or not on their game.

Frank passed away in his 60s due to family generational heart disease leaving his son, Joe and daughter, April to take over the business. Years later they have grown the business mostly by using Frank's model and adding the new generation technology and daily focus on details by streamlining the company.

Meet Jimmy

Jim is a businessman who partnered with a Super Bowl champion who retired from an NFL football team. Many of Jim's clients were seen on the golf course playing alongside the celebrity sports pro and very excited to ask about the legendary plays he experienced. When Jim walks into a restaurant or bar, he is open to all as if he knew everyone, even strangers. It is common for Jim to buy drinks for total strangers who don't remain strangers for long. Jim always goes "top shelf" wherever he goes for lunch, dinner, travel, or business. He knows all too well you can't close business deals or meet top quality friend in a fast food chains or back alley bars. Instead he goes to jazz clubs, steak houses, or seafood restaurants where the exciting people hang out. Jim projects sincerity by asking about your personal life, goals, and family. His genuine concern penetrates the otherwise hard shell of emotional armor we often wear all day. You can see it in his eyes, handshake, and casual pat on the back. Jim places a lot on "personal responsibility". Emphasizing that your word is most important when getting projects done on time and correctly. This includes planning golf outings to engineering projects. Jim has the wealth and material possessions but elects to use this personal approach of sincere respect while finding out what excites each person and projecting belief in them. The control aspect was natural, they remembered him and came back to see him often.

Meet Tony

While in Fort Lauderdale, Florida, my family was hungry for pizza. I knew of a pizza shop nearby and was told it was a great place to go and meet Tony with his secret recipe. When I walked into the pizza shop, I was greeted gingerly by what I later found to be the shop owner, Tony. He asked how we wanted our pizza. I asked what makes his pizza different. He said it was the bottled water and pointed at the water cooler.

I tried a glass of the water and responded, "This doesn't taste like pizza water."

He quickly responded, "It is part of my secret formula"

I bantered back, "It's no longer a secret."

At this point he rifled through a drawer and said he was going to shoot me. He then pulled out a camera and snapped my picture. "The next time you are back, your picture will on the 'customer wall of fame' with your name and where you are from. You will get the opportunity to sign the picture with a pen and make a comment as to how great the pizza tastes."

I return often to the pizza shop to exchange banter with Tony, knowing that every time I walk in, he will have an exciting conversation with me and other customers. He appears to take pride in insulting, questioning, and just engaging with customers. Tony would cut up small samples and ask customers to taste test each. Each had a different topping. You never knew what you were going to taste test. Some samples were excellent, others were terrible, but we all felt like we were contributing something to the outcome of future pizza selections on the menu. His loyalty card would have a hole punched in it each time you returned. After ten holes, you received a free pizza. He kept all the regular's birthdays and anniversary dates on file. When you came in on the date, you got a free pizza. Other times he would offer free sodas or breadsticks while waiting. He kept balloons and candy on hand for children visitors. During sports season, he kept a betting pool. Winners were posted on the bulletin board. You never knew what he was going to do next. It kept all coming back for more. Needless to say, he has doubled this pizza shop size over the years. First by renaming the shop after himself, then engaging in great conversation and new experiences with each customer. All come back to talk with Tony. Once again, the formula, excitement with the banter, belief with good pizza, and control with pictures and handshake followed by, "See you again soon."

Meet Jeff

Jeff was working at age twenty-five in an average occupation as a sales representative for office machine sales. He lived in an apartment in Baltimore, Maryland and had the usual group of friends and acquaintances. One day he made a first step in a series of decisions that began to set into motion the change from an average lifestyle to an exciting lifestyle. It took three to five years to make a complete transition in his lifestyle and add friends and experiences. Jeff had saved enough money to put a down payment on a thirty-two foot Hunter Vision sail boat. Up until this point he knew very little about sailing, with only a few experiences on small sailboats used for training classes on small lakes in the area. His plan was to live on the boat at a marina. The boat was moderate in size with a small bathroom (head), kitchen (galley) dining, and sleeping area. To add to the excitement, he chose a dock that was located in the sailing capital of the East Coast, Annapolis, Maryland. The marina was positioned in the heart of the historic and tourist area of town. Standing on the dock you could see the historic capitol dome, church steeples, drawbridge, and many historical restaurants and pubs. You would think the cost for this endeavor would be high, but surprisingly the budget was not much more than renting an apartment in the same area. Apartment rent was matched with the sailboat payment and docking fees. Other a period of time, he learned how to sail the boat and become good as skipper of the sail boat. During the next few years he become excited and passionate about sailing and entered a casual Wednesday night racing event called the "beer can" races sponsored by the local yacht club. While researching the market, he uncovered a local Navy shipyard that had donated sailboats for auction. He acquired what was a very fast old boat for its size and class. With the encouragement of his new sailing friends, he entered the boat into a weekly race held by the same sailing club. At the same time, his exciting lifestyle carried over into his profession and he became a medical representative selling and helping doctors with operating procedures in hospitals for replacing ankles, hips, and small extremities. They, along with his friends, loved to go sailing on hot sunny days enjoying the racing and occasional trips around the Chesapeake Bay. Soon after he was asked to join the prestigious yacht club and was sponsored as a member. It wasn't long after he met a girl on a Sunday sailing trip. A few years later, they married. He now has many new friends and two daughters who also enjoy sailing. He has sold, brokered, and taught sailing to others over the years.

It just takes one step at a time to move forward into changes in our lives. This is a perfect example of how excitement about a sport (sailing) can become a part of a growing lifestyle. How often do we stay in our velvet rut which is often described as a grave with both ends kicked out? Like Jeff, this may be the time to chase that exciting hobby, dream, or part time business. This is how excitement in a hobby became a lifestyle, belief and trust that it will bring rewards and friends along the way. Control by owning a sailboat and sharing it with others. At time of print, his two girls are actively learning and competing in sailing competitions.

Meet Devin (an exception to the Excitement, Belief, Control program)

Devin was an exceptional student in high school. He excelled in all of his classes and was in the top 10 in the entire state for College SAT scores. As a result, he was accepted with full scholarship in Carnegie Mellon University. Moving ahead he earned his Engineering Degree and Medical Doctorate Degree as a neurosurgeon.

After graduating he was offered a job with a private surgery center and become a partner with all the rewards and benefits of a great career. The key element to his success, transitioning from a middle income community to a top socio-economic level was his high academic performance. This obviously changed his lifestyle and influence in the medical field by helping doctors in his pier group and patients who needed his skills. Along with the educational background he was able to learn to fly an airplane, golf and travel extensively with his family. As a side note, he did meet a Registered Nurse in the operating room who appreciated the Excitement, Belief and Control aspect of his lifestyle and character. They live happily with four children who are following their footsteps.

Very few people excel academically in education, music, sports, etc. You could say the excitement is the gifted talent, belief is the milestones they achieved and control is their discipline to stick with the goal.

Meet Senior Leaders and Jack

I have singled out a special category that requires a different approach - the senior age leaders in the business, work and social community. This is a group starting at age 50 but more concentrated on 65 to 90. Most of these seniors have a very high energy and project the excitement, trust and control aspect with a unique approach tailored to age. I singled out this group because it is an elite person who often can go by a difference set of rules. In general a more mature leader is perceived as having more experience in the school of hard knocks. This is evident in the age of our president, congress leaders and legislators we see on TV. As you study this group, you realize they don't become upset as easily and have better control when directly confronted. They also know how to handle a 'no' response, having heard it so many times. This includes cross examining character, company, products, services, policies usually tied to overall trust. This may be tied to the emotional connection younger career people have toward their parents, teachers, ministers and mentors. Added are older leaders that have the experience of being on the front firing line and knowing the sniper shots that they have fielded thru the years. They also have the 'good old boys' sense of humor and wisdom. They have simply learned to stay cool under fire. Jack is a friend who is in his senior years. His motto is 'hard work, good food, fine wine and great friends. Coupled with this are his years and years of networking connections with a history of mutual trust. Jack knows who in the business community has performed. He has a second sense in spotting the con artists, liars and exaggerators. Jack is part of a close networked business community or in a vertical occupation such as construction, medical field or specialty product sales and service. This group exchanges confidential information freely but with trust." This winning talent that Jack has is only achieved by years of experience. To quote the singer, Kenny Rogers, "You got to know when to hold em and know when to fold em" This is why Jack is so valuable in the corporate community. He has value in the business community with a much later retirement. So what do we do when we encounter an older business leader? The best approach is to relate to a relative of close age or a mentor of the same age. Statements such as, "You remind me of my uncle who mentored me for many years' This followed by a story that uncle Joe shared helps. As far as Jack's statement about the food, fine wine and great re-lationships – Jack makes sure he brings the potential team leader into an evening at a fine restaurant. This is where the emotional connection and trust are de-veloped. Jack simply wants to know what your desires are to make the deal work. Once he finds your passion and desire, he has accomplished the excite-ment and trust portion of the deal. After an agreement for the deal is made, he usually leaves the control factor up to the younger staff to work out the details. He does make sure he stays at the helm and watches the details worked out. A deal can easily be derailed during details which is the control aspect of the trans-action. I important paradigm Jack follows - for some reason the deal goes sour, Jack knows to continue with the friendship, excitement and trust because another opportunity may come up in the future.

Remembering names: Most people we meet say, "I have trouble remember-ing names". One of the key reasons for not remembering names (aside from lower IQ) is that we are not excited about the person we are meeting. We're really not interested in them. Solution – find something exciting about each person we meet to the point that we want to follow up with them as long term friends. If you can't find something exciting about the person we met, maybe it is a good thing to forget their name.

Transferring excitement, belief and control into a club or organization. Ever think about starting a club or organization with a great cause? How would you go about making this goal a success? In 1991 I started a chamber of com-merce. This organization grew over the 30 plus years mainly because we used the Excitement, belief and control factor. The organization now has over 8,000 subscribers and 10,000 readers of our quarterly publication. Go to www.south-pointechamber.com for more information.

Here are the basic steps.

1. Focus excitement, energy, and goals on individual members. If it's fishing, have members take turns speaking on different techniques and waterways for catching fish. If it's business, focus on lead generation and show and tell. If it's cooking, focus on sharing recipes. If it's sports, focus on individual training and shared exercise routines. You get the idea.

2. For belief and trust, watch the group grow. That is the best report card on success.

3. For control, determine realistic rules, membership fees, and awards so all will come back for another rewarding experience. Couple all of this with group events, member plaques, trophies, recognition with titles and name badges for events.

Excitement, Trust, and Control and setting the meeting environment.
It's important to select the right meeting locations. When choosing your meeting location, much depends on the agenda and goals to be accomplished during the meeting time. For the sake of this exercise, we will assume this is a product or service presentation meeting to a prospective new client. Choosing a location is our first step. Many feel there is a balance between picking a casual loose atmosphere such as a sports restaurant bar verses a bank boardroom. It is our contention that the 'upscale' locations are best suited for sales presentations. These are not always the most expensive locations, but the upscale locations bring on a transfer of credibility by association with the product or service. Often banks offer their offices or boardrooms to regular clients. Most upscale restaurants have private dining rooms available for lunch at menu prices. Country club restaurants work fine especially during off season when golfers or swimmers are not using the facility. Many four and five star hotels

have meeting rooms at no additional cost if you are catering a lunch. Often upscale hotels have open lobbies with private seating areas for presentations. Worst case, be prepared to pay for the facility unless your existing office is on par with the above mentioned facilities, don't use it. Remember, we are looking for excitement. In contrast, never meet at a fast food chain, pizza shop, or sandwich shop. If your office is not up to par, it is not a problem to announce to your prospective client that you have a change in location. This is perfectly acceptable, especially for a lunch meeting. Don't forget to have name badges so all will see who they are meeting. Make sure the company name or position is included on the badge.

Now let's take a close look at the meeting room. First check the basics. Is the temperature comfortable? To hot or cold is very distracting. Check lighting. Make sure all lighting is operational. Ideally you want to control the lighting to change the mood during the meeting – especially if you are using a TV monitor or projector. Make sure you have adequate electrical plugs in the right locations and check that they are operational. Nothing turns off a meeting agenda like having no power for computers or blanked out computer with a dying battery. When making a presentation it is best to work using a professional presentation program. This gives you control of the presentation as you move from subject to subject via picture changes. It is best to show the image on a large screen TV or projector. Remember that bigger vivid pictures are more exciting to watch and hold the audience's attention. When using handouts, don't give the full presentation to the client at the beginning of the meeting. They tend to read ahead and once again, you lose control. Instead hand pages to your client one at a time as the next subject or concept comes into play. Color pictures are always worth a thousand words. Invest in a digital camera or good smart phone and take pictures of your past and present clients and projects. People will remember the pictures long after the dialogue. Make sure you print the pictures or slides and hand them out afterword. In general, keep the presentation under thirty minutes. There is nothing more boring than a long, drawn out meeting. In general, talk clearly and move from one concept to another quickly. Allow time for feedback for questions from the client. If a questions asked and covered further on in the presentation, just respond. It will save time if you wait for that answer later in the presentation. Remember to take a ten minute break after thirty minutes, announcing that the question and answer period is to follow.

The time for the meeting can be as important as the location. Always go for a 11 AM time with a rollover into lunch. There is something magical about breaking bread with clients (or friends). It opens up the lines of communications. Now let's review the meeting high points.

1. Pick an exciting location. Pick a location that is fresh, new, upscale, and interesting.

2. Project belief by choosing a financially solid location and Power Point or short video presentation, preferably on a large screen.

3. Keep control of the time by having a meeting rollover into lunch or cocktail hour.

During lunch, I usually keep the topic light and try to get to know the client's personal likes and dislikes. Stay off the topics of religion and politics unless you know for certain your beliefs align. Asking how the family is doing, hobbies, school for kids and sports are a safe bet. Guys love to talk about old cars. Try to listen eighty percent of the time during this venture but do interject information. After the luncheon, make sure to thank all those in attendance for spending time with you. Highlight any information that you owe them, for example specifications documents, pictures, etc. It is very important to establish the next meeting date, telephone call time, or email correspondence. This helps to keep the next step in your control and lends an importance to the program. Beware when you hear time commitments that are open-ended. Examples would be, "We'll call you with questions after reviewing the information" Correct this by saying, "I'll pencil in a telephone call around Wednesday next week if that is okay with you." Make sure you call when scheduled or your credibility to follow-up will be lost. Don't be afraid to ask the client how they feel about your product and or service and what is their timeline for making a decision. Finish up with a follow-up email or letter. This should highlight the points of concern, issues raised, and solutions. Just a point on dress code. This was addressed earlier in the book under the belief section. Shirts should always have our company name embroidered on the pocket. If possible, hand out ink pens and note pads with matching company logo.

SUMMARY

We have provided the tools to help you stay on track with the excitement, trust and control programs. We have provided the tools to help you stay on track with the excitement, trust (belief) and control aspect when with friends, business associates, or even while meeting strangers.

1. Practice talking faster or more concisely without rambling or repeating yourself.

2. Change subjects if you find you are not holding interest. Watch for clients glancing at phones, looking off into a distance or flipping thru papers.

3. Stay current on the news, sports, etc. Automobiles are great common denominators for men. Talk about children and families.

4. Keep your surroundings such as clothing, office, and automobile fresh and exciting.

5. Take detailed notes on all you do. Be sure to provide copies or your meeting notes to all who attend as a reinforcement and reminder.

6. Pay attention to details and names. That alone will impress others around you.

7. Remember events and past conversations in detail.

8. Talk about future plans and how to accomplish them.

9. Pick good conversation topics that are exciting.

    For couples, How did the two of you met?

    Where are you planning your next vacation?

    What hobbies or sports do you like?

    Keep a calendar for appointment, etc.

    Don't exaggerate, think before you make a statement and make sure it rings true.

    Always back up your word with action or keep quiet.

10. Is someone is confronting you about an issue or subject? Make a friendly bet as to who is right. Let's bet a steak dinner on that.

A word about Impatience and anger. We often get angry about the smallest issues. How often have we gotten anxious over these details. Traffic light staying red too long? Waiting at a ticket counter too long? Stuck in traffic? Waiting for a slow teller at the bank? When you feel your anxiety level rising, try these steps.

1. Mentally step back and watch the situation as if it were a movie script and you are one of the actors.

2. Ask yourself, "What is really going on here?"

3. Many times the simple process of watching is entertaining in itself.

4. Why is the person holding things up?

5. How can you improve on the situation?

6. How do you avoid getting into the same trap in the future?

Many times we are harboring resentment and can't put our finger on what's causing the anxiety. Are we angry at the long red light or are we really angry because we left the house late? Are we angry at the red light or are we angry about the mission (or job) we are on? It's interesting to self examine what is really taking place. If a person is holding you up or confronting you, here is a simple rule that will keep you in control.

Be patient but firmly state your case without an attitude in your manner-isms, gestures, voice tone, or actions. Let the person know you are watching the situation closely and that you are acutely aware of what is taking place. This in itself will often correct the problem. Always remember to be kind and patient while stating our case. The other person is watching for a reason to justify their position. Statements such as, "I was wrong but he had a xxx atti-tude" allows the person to keep fighting with you. Speak up firmly but with patience, kindness while letting them know you are watching the situation closely works best. Remember, if you want to say something, say it, but with kindness, patience and, firmness. Laughing at the situation works, but be care-ful not to appear to be mocking or cynical in our voice tone and gestures. You will find that speaking your mind can be fun, it gives you a good release, and lets others know what you are thinking. Keeping things pent up often raises your blood pressure and stress. Later, evaluate the situation and make sure you take detailed notes so that you don't get in that situation again. In public restaurants and stores and services, note which places are more efficient and what are best day or time to attend. Sometimes it is worth paying a little more to stay away from inefficient staff and facilities. Try calling ahead by using the smart phone services and products. This opens our options while accomplishing our goals.

NOTES

NOTES

Chapter Four
Conclusion

I hope that this book has been helpful for you. Whether you are making a bold business move or just trying to get through a routine day, The EX-CITEMENT, BELIEF (TRUST) AND CONTROL factors will make goals easier for you and your friends. This approach should be fun and relaxing. Try not to be too critical of yourself and others. As we grow a little more in character and efficiency, wait and see how life becomes easier with each step. If you have goals to reach in life, you will see how much easier they are to achieve. If you have all you want, use these steps to help others. In life, balance is most often the key to success. Use the Excitement, Belief, Control format coupled with outspokenness, firmness, kindness, and patience. How can you lose? I suggest you print these three words on paper and tape it to you bathroom mirror, kitchen, cell phone, desktop, or car dashboard. If anything else, it will keep you motivated each moment of the day.

END

Thank you for reading. Please contact me at dhodor@southpointe.net or call 724-873-7777. Ext 22.

NOTES

NOTES

NOTES